EARLY BIRD STORIES

Our Place in Space

An Alien's Guide

Alex Francis

Early ★ Reader

Lerner Publications ◆ Minneapolis

First American edition published in 2020 by Lerner Publishing Group, Inc.

An original concept by Alex Francis
Copyright © 2021 Alex Francis

Illustrated by Alex Francis

First published by Maverick Arts Publishing Limited

Maverick
arts publishing

Licensed Edition
Our Place in Space: An Alien's Guide

For the avoidance of doubt, pursuant to Chapter 4 of the Copyright, Designs and Patents Act of 1988, the proprietor asserts the moral right of the Author to be identified as the author of the Work; and asserts the moral right of the Author to be identified as the illustrator of the Work.

All US rights reserved. No part of this book may be reproduced, stored in a retrieval system, or transmitted in any form or by any means—electronic, mechanical, photocopying, recording, or otherwise—without the prior written permission of Lerner Publishing Group, Inc., except for the inclusion of brief quotations in an acknowledged review.

Lerner Publications Company
An imprint of Lerner Publishing Group, Inc.
241 First Avenue North
Minneapolis, MN 55401 USA

For reading levels and more information, look up this title at www.lernerbooks.com.

Main body text set in Mikado. Typeface provided by HVD Fonts.

Library of Congress Cataloging-in-Publication Data
Names: Francis, Alex (Graphic novel writer), author, illustrator.
Title: Our place in space : an alien's guide / Alex Francis.
Description: First American edition. | Minneapolis : Lerner Publications, 2021. | Series:
  Early bird nonfiction readers – silver | "First published by Maverick Arts Publishing
  Limited." | Audience: Ages 5–9 | Audience: Grades 2–3 | Summary: "Earth is just
  one of eight planets in the solar system. Finn and Zeek, two aliens from another
  world, guide readers around the sun, the planets, and what lies beyond Neptune"—
  Provided by publisher.
Identifiers: LCCN 2020002949 (print) | LCCN 2020002950 (ebook) |
  ISBN 9781728415109 (library binding) | ISBN 9781728415161 (paperback) |
  ISBN 9781728415178 (ebook)
Subjects: LCSH: Planets—Juvenile literature. | Solar system—Juvenile literature.
Classification: LCC QB501.3 .F73 2021 (print) | LCC QB501.3 (ebook) | DDC 523.2—
  dc23

LC record available at https://lccn.loc.gov/2020002949
LC ebook record available at https://lccn.loc.gov/2020002950

Manufacured in the United States of America
1-48666-49089-1/13/2020

Table of Contents

Dear Finn and Zeek,

I want to visit Earth, but I'm having some trouble finding my way there. The solar system has so many planets and **moons!**

Can you please explain the solar system so I can find Earth?

From,
Zoomy
(Planet Faraway)

Introduction

The solar system is the **planetary system** that humans live in. It is one of over 2,500 in the **Milky Way.** There are still more to discover. Space is huge!

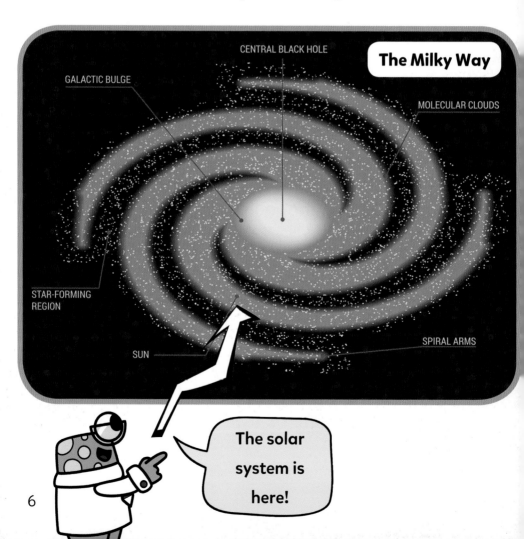

CENTRAL BLACK HOLE

The Milky Way

GALACTIC BULGE

MOLECULAR CLOUDS

STAR-FORMING REGION

SUN

SPIRAL ARMS

The solar system is here!

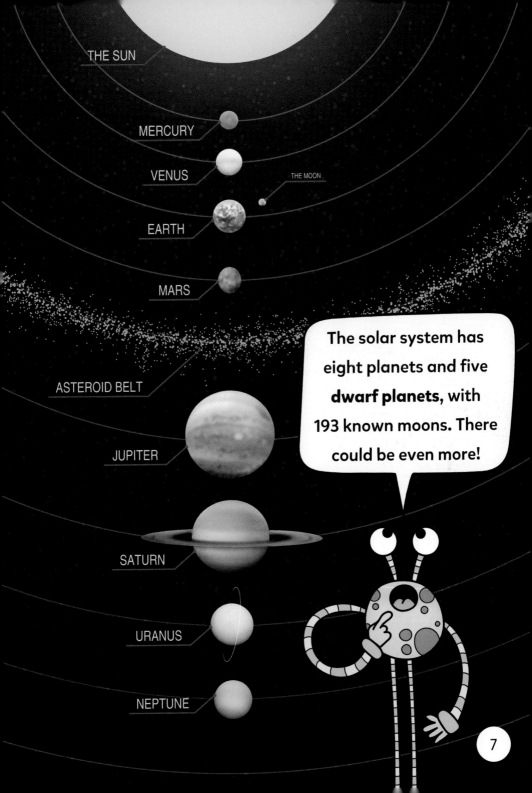

THE SUN

MERCURY

VENUS

THE MOON

EARTH

MARS

ASTEROID BELT

JUPITER

The solar system has eight planets and five **dwarf planets,** with 193 known moons. There could be even more!

SATURN

URANUS

NEPTUNE

The Sun

The sun is known as a **dwarf star** and is a sphere of superhot gas. It releases lots of heat and light! We see it in the sky during the day, but not at night.

The sun is 109 times bigger than Earth and much heavier!

The sun is the star at the center of the solar system. The sun is so massive and has such strong **gravity** that planets **orbit** it even when they're really far away.

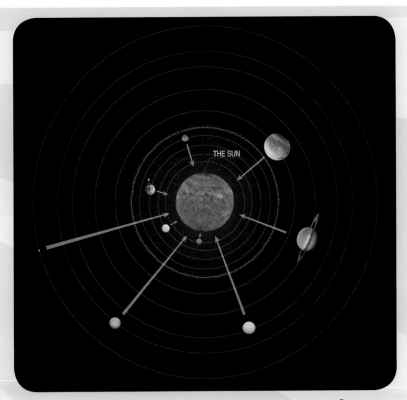

THE SUN

Some planets have stronger gravity than others. You would feel very heavy if you visited them!

Terrestrial Planets

Mercury

The terrestrial planets are the four planets closest to the sun. They have solid, rocky surfaces.

Mercury

Mercury is the closest planet to the sun and is also the smallest in the solar system. It gets very hot in the day but very cold at night, ranging from about -292°F (-180°C) to 806°F (430°C)! It takes just under 88 days to orbit the sun.

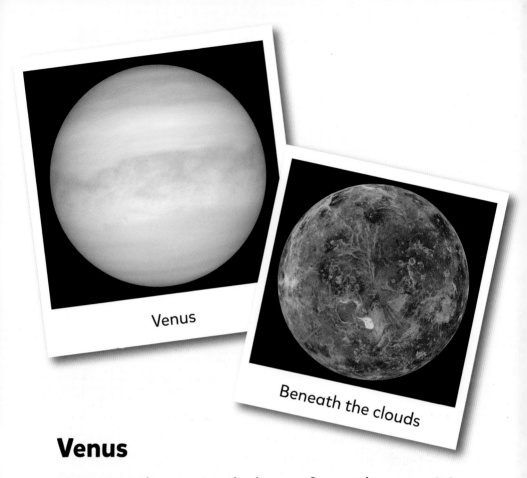

Venus

Beneath the clouds

Venus

Venus is the second planet from the sun. It's the hottest planet in the solar system, with an average temperature of 864°F (462°C)! The surface is covered with thick clouds. Venus takes almost 225 days to orbit the sun. It is strange because it rotates in the opposite direction most other planets do!

Moon

Earth

Earth is the only planet known to have life. It's the third planet from the sun, and one orbit takes 365 days. This makes one year.

Earth has one moon. Most scientists think the moon formed around 4.5 billion years ago, when another planet called Theia collided with Earth.

The Earth is also special for being in the "Goldilocks Zone," a special distance from the sun that is just right for liquid water. It's not too hot and not too cold. It's just right for life!

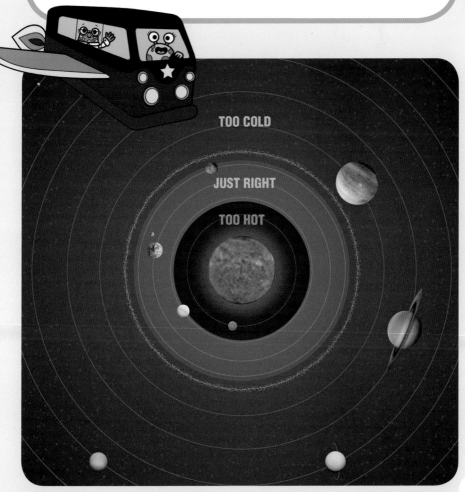

TOO COLD

JUST RIGHT

TOO HOT

Mars

Mars is also known as the Red Planet, and it's the fourth planet from the sun. It looks red because its soil contains iron oxide, which is red in color.

Mars has temperatures ranging from around -225°F (-143°C) to 95°F (35°C). Frozen water has been found on the planet. Mars has two moons, Phobos and Deimos. Mars is also home to Olympus Mons, the biggest volcano in the entire solar system!

The Asteroid Belt

The asteroid belt is a ring of thousands of asteroids between Mars and Jupiter. Asteroids are made from bits of metal and rocky material. There is one dwarf planet in the asteroid belt called Ceres.

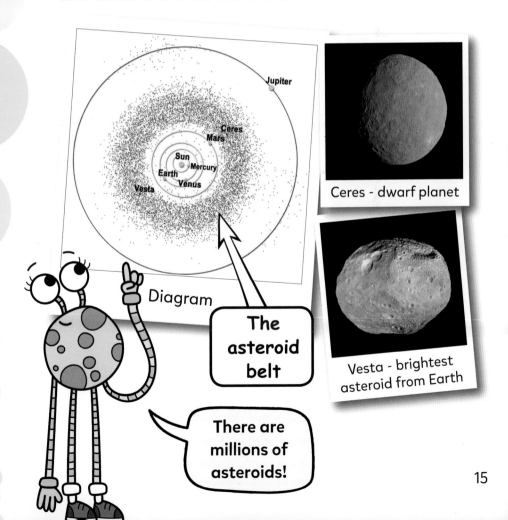

Diagram

The asteroid belt

Ceres - dwarf planet

Vesta - brightest asteroid from Earth

There are millions of asteroids!

Gas Giants

Jupiter

Gas giants are made mostly of gas, so you wouldn't be able to stand on the surface. They are thought to have small, solid cores.

The Great Red Spot

Jupiter is the biggest planet in the solar system. The surface of Jupiter always changes because all of the gases are swirling around really fast. One of its most famous features is the Great Red Spot, which is a storm larger than Earth!

So far, 79 moons have been discovered orbiting Jupiter! Jupiter's gravity is so strong that it causes some moons to stretch.

The largest moons of Jupiter are called the Galilean moons. These are Io, Europa, Ganymede, and Callisto. Ganymede is the largest moon in the whole solar system!

The Great Red Spot has been shrinking since it was discovered. Some scientists think it will disappear one day!

Saturn

Saturn is a smaller gas giant than Jupiter.
It is the second largest planet in the solar
system. Saturn's north and south poles
have huge storms. The one at the north
pole is shaped like a hexagon!

Saturn's best-known feature is its rings, which are mostly made of small bits of ice, rock, and dust. It has at least 62 moons. The largest is called Titan.

Ice Giants

Ice giants are very similar to gas giants, but they also have a lot of ice.

Uranus

Uranus is extremely cold, with a minimum temperature of around -371°F (-224°C)!

Uranus has 27 known moons and 13 rings, but the rings are smaller and harder to see than Saturn's. The outside of the planet is made of water, ammonia, and the methane ice crystals that make it look pale blue. Uranus is very strange because it rotates on its side!

Neptune

Neptune is the farthest known planet in the solar system. It takes almost 165 years for it to make one trip around the sun! It has 14 known moons and looks blue.

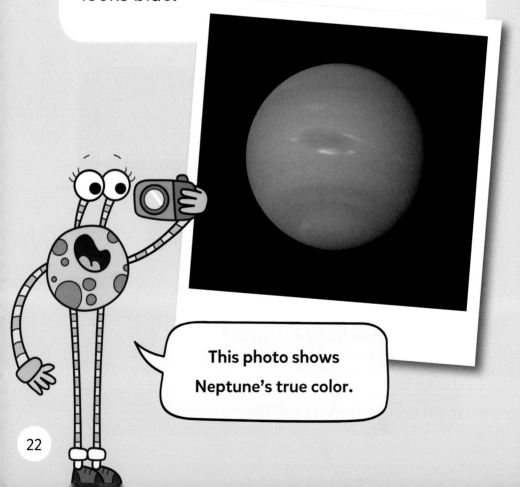

This photo shows Neptune's true color.

Neptune has very faint rings!

Neptune is very windy! Even if you could stand on Neptune, the wind would blow you away! Even though it is much farther from the sun, it's roughly as cold as Uranus.

Whoa! The wind is dangerously fast!

Pluto

Pluto used to be known as the ninth planet of the solar system, but it does not have enough gravity. It has now been renamed a dwarf planet. Pluto is farther from the sun than Neptune and has five known moons. It's very small and very far away. One trip around the sun takes Pluto about 248 years!

That bit looks like a heart!

Beyond the Solar System

Voyager 1 was launched by **NASA** in 1977, and on August 25, 2012, it became the first spacecraft to travel beyond the solar system. It carries a golden disk with greetings from Earth and information about the human race, just in case it comes into contact with **alien** life.

Good luck, *Voyager 1*!

Preparing the golden disk

That's how Zeek and I discovered Earth!

MESSAGE SENT

Dear Zoomy,

The solar system has eight major planets. To find Earth, look for the biggest planet (Jupiter). Then go through the asteroid belt, past the red planet (Mars), and then you should see Earth! It's the third planet from the sun.

Look out for **satellites** and the International Space Station orbiting Earth!

From,
Finn and Zeek

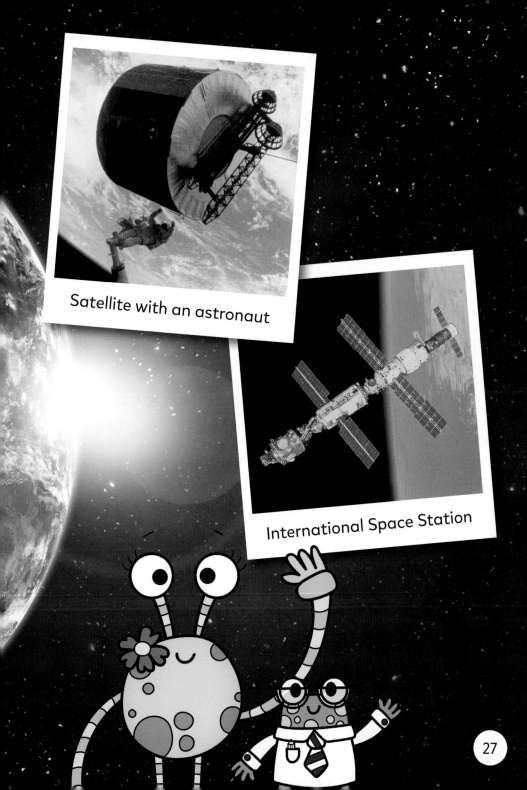

Satellite with an astronaut

International Space Station

Quiz

1. What is the sun?
   a) A bright asteroid
   b) A dwarf star
   c) A giant star

2. What are the four solid planets closest to the sun called?
   a) Terrific planets
   b) Tougher planets
   c) Terrestrial planets

3. What is this called?
   a) The Great Red Spot
   b) The Big Blob
   c) Jupiter

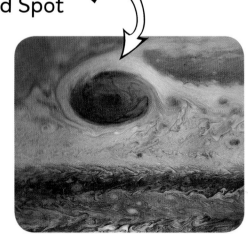

4. Uranus is . . . ?

  a) An ice giant

  b) A gas giant

  c) A moon

5. What is the weather like on Neptune?

  a) Wet

  b) Hot

  c) Windy

6. What is *Voyager 1* carrying?

  a) Plants

  b) People

  c) A golden disk

Quiz Answers:
1b, 2c, 3a, 4a, 5c, 6c

Glossary

alien: life from somewhere other than Earth

dwarf planets: planets whose gravity is not strong enough to clear the surrounding area of space

dwarf star: a relatively small star

gravity: a force that draws objects toward one another

Milky Way: the spiral galaxy containing our solar system

moons: natural objects orbiting a planet, dwarf planet, or asteroid

NASA: abbreviation for the National Aeronautics and Space Administration, which is in charge of the US space program and carries out aeronautics and aerospace research

orbit: a repeating path that an object in space takes around another

planetary system: a group of planets or asteroids that orbit one or more stars

satellites: small objects that orbit a larger object in space

Index

Leveled for Guided Reading

Early Bird Stories have been edited and leveled by leading educational consultants to correspond with guided reading levels. The levels are assigned by taking into account the content, language style, layout, and phonics used in each book.

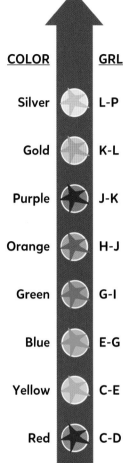

COLOR	GRL
Silver	L-P
Gold	K-L
Purple	J-K
Orange	H-J
Green	G-I
Blue	E-G
Yellow	C-E
Red	C-D
Pink	A-C